1

**How the Babylonian Flood
Became the Story of the Great Deluge in the Bible.
(And How Utnapishtim Became Noah).**

**Synopsis and Translation of the Sumerian, Akkadian,
and Assyrian Cuneiform Tablets**

Excerpts from

Are we worshiping a fake god?
How Babylonian and Phoenician Gods Became Yahweh and the god of Christians!

First Edition, published in 1963, in French, in France.
Second Edition, published in 2008, in English, under the title "Anunnaki Greatest Secrets Revealed by the Phoenicians and Ulema: Are we worshiping a fake God?" in the United States, ISBN: 978-1438215921.
Third Edition, published in 2013, in the United States, in two formats: a) Paperback, b)Amazon Kindle Edition.

***   ***   ***

Date of Publication: July 23, 2014
Published by Times Square Press, WJNA, Inc., New York and Berlin.

Website of the author:
www.maximilliendelafayettebibliography.org/biblio
Contact: Marla Cohen at newyorkgate@aol.com

Maximillien de Lafayette

HOW THE BABYLONIAN FLOOD BECAME THE STORY OF THE GREAT DELUGE IN THE BIBLE.

**How the Babylonian Flood
Became the Story of the Great Deluge in the Bible.
(And How Utnapishtim Became Noah).**

**Synopsis and Translation of the Sumerian, Akkadian,
and Assyrian Cuneiform Tablets**

Maximillien de Lafayette

***   ***   ***

Times Square Press
New York   Berlin   Paris   Madrid
2014

Table Of Contents

- Characteristics and dissimilarities of the three Babylonian versions of the story of the flood, the Epic of Gilgamesh and Berossus' account.
- The Sumerian story of the flood according to Berossus, a priest of the cult of Marduk in Babylon.
- The Babylonian story of the Flood and the Biblical account of the Deluge were mentioned on a tablet from Ugarit.

*** *** ***

One picture is worth a 1,000 words.

Hebrews worshipping the Anunnaki-Sumerian god Ea.
Abraham was one of the early Hebrews who worshipped Ea.
This was confirmed on numerous Sumerian, Assyrian, Akkadian, Babylonian,
Syrian and Phoenician tablets, seals and coins
found in Eridu, Ur of the Chaldees, Ugarit, Babylon,
and the Syrian town of Ebla.

———————————————————

Introduction
Biblical stories taken from much older religions.

97% of the Bible is pure fabrication, and almost 95% of the major Biblical stories are copied from Phoenician, Ugaritic, Syrian-Canaanite, Mesopotamian and Egyptian myths, poems, texts and stories, <u>written centuries before the Bible was crafted.</u>

Although the Bible is a majestic and a superb piece of literature nourished with wisdom, and conveying remarkable ethical and moral messages and lessons, the Bible is by no means, the word of God, or an original Hebraic work.
And beyond the shadow of a doubt, Yahweh (Jehovah) is a recast, and an amalgam of pagans' gods ; the gods of Mesopotamia, Phoenicia and Ugarit.

Numerous historians, archaeologists, linguists, scholars and anthropology's forensic scientists agree that the Bible's most formidable and colorful stories such as:
1-The Tower of Babel,
2-Genesis,
3-Adam and Eve,
4-Garden of Eden,
5-The Great Flood (To name a few)
were taken from Mesopotamian, Ugaritic, Phoenician, Canaanite, Egyptian, Assyrian, Akkadian, and Chaldean myths, and epics recorded on ancient clay tablets and slabs, centuries before the Bible was written, and the name and the presence of God , or more exactly one God, were known to the Israelites/Early Hebrews.
In fact, the name of God "Yahweh", his attributes and extraordinary (Supernatural) powers and deeds were borrowed from pagans' gods; gods the Israelites worshiped before they "created" their own god "Yahweh", who

centuries later, became the God of the Christians and the Muslims.

In this short treatise, we will analyze and explain the origin of the Biblical story of the Flood (Great Deluge), and how the Hebrews took the story of the Flood from the Babylonian texts (A much older story), while they were in exile in Babylon.

Today, and after I have spent 55 years studying comparative religions and learning from the Honorable Anunnaki Ulema, and arguing metaphysical and theological subjects with sheiks, imams, bishops, priests and archbishops, I can tell you that many of Islam's stories and "visions" (Sorat, Rou'ya) were inspired by Christianity, and Christianity's tales and prophetic events were taken from Judaism, and Judaism's fabulous stories, revelations and teachings were copied from much older religions' texts, fables, myths and stories.

My statements and findings are based upon the Akkadian, Sumerian, and Assyrian cuneiform clay tablets found in Babylon and Nineveh.
I am reproducing in the this short treatise, the original Mesopotamian texts, and my translation of these texts, and comparing them word-for-word, with the Biblical texts, to prove beyond the shadow of a doubt that the Biblical story of the Flood was taken from the Mesopotamian story of the Great Deluge, which appeared on clay tablets, centuries before the Bible was written!!

I encourage you to read the Mesopotamian myths/stories of Utnapishtim, Gilgamesh, Adapa, Enkidu, and the Babylonian story of the Great Deluge, so you could find for yourself that all these Mesopotamian stories appeared in the Bible almost verbatim with minor colorful variations and a clever twist.

Although, the Hebrews invented few and new divine concepts, they remained "compilers" of much old stories;

they just took old ones and added a new twist, as did before them, several Middle and Near Eastern civilizations.
This practice was/is a trademark of the religions of the ancient world and vanished civilizations.

They simply compiled old stories and myths and added uniquely colorful and well-crafted new twists, for various and obvious reasons such as:

- 1-To meet their geo-political needs.
- 2-To accomplish, protect and preserve their purposes and objectives.
- 3-To create a new national entity and pride for their God.
- 4-To justify their savage occupation of new lands (Canaan) and the destruction of cities and towns by the name of God (Yahweh) who gave them the right to do so!

*** *** ***

The Babylonian Story of the Flood Versus the Biblical Story of the Flood.

There is a difference of approximately 600 years between the Babylonian flood and the Biblical flood.

Worth mentioning here that archaeologists discovered sediments and deposits of a flood in the Mesopotamian region which occurred in 2900 B.C., and concluded that the flood was indeed the flooding of the Euphrates river.
According to historians and scholars, the Biblical flood occurred circa 2300 B.C.

There is a difference of approximately 600 years between the Babylonian flood and the Biblical flood. It is very clear that the Hebrew scribes borrowed the story of the Great Flood from the Mesopotamians.
The earliest story of the flood appeared in the "Epic of Atrahasis" and was recorded on three clay tablets during the reign of Babylonian king Ammi-saduga, 1647-1626 B.C.
A second story of the Babylonian flood appeared in the "Epic of Gilgamesh", circa 1100 B.C.

*** *** ***

Note:
The Sumero-Akkadian-Assyrian words: "Pir-napishtim", "Utnapishtim", and "Ziusudra", (Atrahasis in Greek) correspond to:
1-The Biblical Noah.
2-Nouh (Nuh) in Arabic.
3-Nuh in Turkish.
4-Nuh (Nuuh) in Farsi (Persian).
5-Nuh in Urdu.
6-Noach in Hebrew.

17

7-Noach in Tiberian.

Same stories in the Babylonian texts and the Bible.

Excerpts from the Mesopotamian texts, word-for-word, and my translation:

From the Mesopotamian tablet: Line 8 to line 196:
"God Ea spoke to Utnapishtim (Utnapishtim)
who lived in Shuruppak,
And told him to build a ship
to save himself
And his family from the coming flood."

*** *** ***

1.The Anunnaki god Ea warned Utnapishtim about a flood.
Instructions on how to build the boat.

In the Babylonian epics, god Ea warned Utnapishtim about a flood that will decimate the world and annihilate the human race, and instructed him on how to build a boat to save himself and his family.
In the Bible, God Yahweh told Noah to build an ark of cypress wood and make rooms in it and coat it with pitch inside and out.
Genesis 6:14,
"Build a large boat from cypress wood
And waterproof it with tar,
inside and out.
Then construct decks and
stalls throughout its interior."

Ea even gave Utnapishtim precise instructions on how to build the boat, including height, length, width, etc.

18

The Babylonian tablet provided us with a clear description of the interior of the boat.
The tablet specified that the boat should have six decks and seven levels, and include a divider;
"Dividing the whole interior of the boat
into nine compartments."

In the Bible, Yahweh told Noah the very same thing, and gave him the measurements of a boat he should build to save himself and his family. God told Noah how to make a boat, and gave him precise instructions.

Genesis 6:13,
"And God said to Noah, "I have determined to make
an end of all flesh, for the earth is filled
with violence because of them;
now I am going to destroy them along with the earth."

Genesis 6:14,
"Make yourself an ark of cypress wood;
make rooms in the ark, and cover it
inside and out with pitch."

Genesis 6:15,
"This is how you are to make it:
the length of the ark three hundred cubits,
its width fifty cubits, and its height thirty cubits."

Genesis 6:16,
"Make a roof for the ark,
and finish it to a cubit above;
and put the door of the ark in its side;
make it with lower, second, and third decks."

*** *** ***

19

The biblical vision of Noah and his boat.

The Christians' vision of the Deluge.

In Tablet XI of the "Epic of Gilgamesh", the Anunnaki god Ea spoke to Utnapishtim and said to him:

"Man of Shuruppak, son of Ubar-Tutu,
Tear down the house (Utnapishtim's house)
and build a boat.
Leave behind possessions (Wealth)
and seek the living people
Bring inside the boat,
the seeds of all living creatures.
The dimensions of the boat you shall build
must be equal to each other.
The length of the boat should equal the width of the boat."

*** *** ***

2.Bringing animals to the boat.

God Ea instructed Utnapishtim to bring inside the boat, all the animals he could find around him, wild and not wild. In Tablet XI, passage 35, god Ea said:

"Bring in the sheep inside the boat...
birds, cattle, and the creatures of the land..."

In the Babylonian Atrahasis, we read:

"On board of the boat (Inside the boat),
he brought all the creatures (Animals) of the field."

In the Bible, Genesis 6:19,
"And of every living thing, of all flesh,
you shall bring two of every kind into the ark,
to keep them alive with you;
they shall be male and female."

Genesis 6:20,
"Of the birds according to their kinds,
and of the animals according to their kinds,
of every creeping thing of the ground according to its kind,
two of every kind shall come in to you,
to keep them alive."

Genesis 8:16-17,
"Bring out every kind of living creature...
the birds, the animals, and all the creatures."

Chapter II, Genesis 7:2,
"Take with you seven pairs of all clean animals,
the male and its mate;
and a pair of the animals that are not clean,
the male and its mate..."

Chapter II, Genesis 7:3,

"And seven pairs of the birds of the air also,
male and female, to keep their kind alive
on the face of all the earth."

Chapter II, Genesis 7:8,
"Of clean animals, and of animals
that are not clean, and of birds,
and of everything that creeps on the ground."

Chapter II, Genesis 7:9,
"Two and two, male and female,
went into the ark with Noah,
as God had commanded Noah."

Chapter II, Genesis 7:14,
"They and every wild animal of every kind,
and all domestic animals of every kind,
and every creeping thing that creeps on the earth,
and every bird of every kind,
every bird, every winged creature."

Chapter 9, Genesis 9:10,
"And with every living creature that is with you,
the birds, the domestic animals,
and every animal of the earth with you,
as many as came out of the ark."

*** *** ***

3.The dove.

Another striking similarity between the Babylonian story and the Hebrew story is the mentioning of the dove.
In the Babylonian Tablet XI, we read that a dove was released from the boat to find a dry land, exactly as it is written in the Bible.

Here is an excerpt from the Babylonian text:

"On the seventh day, I released a dove,
the dove flew but came back.
Then I released a swallow,
and the swallow returned.
Then I sent a raven but did not return."

In the Epic of Gilgamesh, line 147, we read:
"I (Utnapishtim) sent forth (out of the boat) a dove.
The dove went off, and came back to me."

 In the Bible, we read:
"He (Noah) sent forth the dove out of the ark,
and the dove came back to him."

In the Babylonian Epic of Gilgamesh, line 153, we read:
"I (Utnapishtim) sent forth a raven."

In the Bible, we learned that Noah sent forth a raven. The Bible told us that Noah released a dove from his boat, and the dove returned to him, and once again he sent off the dove, and when the dove returned to him carrying an olive branch, Noah knew that the dove found a dry land.
Chapter 8, Genesis 8:7,
"And sent out the raven;
and it went to and from until
the waters were dried up from the earth."

Chapter 8, Genesis 8:8,

"Then he sent out the dove from him,
to see if the waters had subsided
from the face of the ground."

Chapter 8, Genesis 8:9,
"But the dove found no place to set its foot,
and it returned to him to the ark,
for the waters were still on the face of the whole earth.
So he put out his hand and took it
and brought it into the ark with him."

Chapter 8, Genesis 8:10,
"He waited another seven days,
and again he sent out the dove from the ark."

Chapter 8, Genesis 8:11,
"And the dove came back to him in the evening,
and there in its beak was a freshly plucked olive leaf;
so Noah knew that the waters
had subsided from the earth."

Chapter 8, Genesis 8:12,
"Then he waited another seven days,
and sent out the dove;
and it did not return to him any more."

*** *** ***

4.The birds are set free:
The Mesopotamian tablet: Lines 145-155: Utnapishtim told us that the birds were set free to find out if the waters receded. In the Bible, Noah too sent a dove to find out if the waters receded.

*** *** ***

5.The boat resting on the top of a mountain:
A passage from the Bible referred to Noah's ark which rested on the top of Mount Ararat, as the flood began to go down.
Chapter 8, Genesis 8:4,
"And in the seventh month,
on the seventeenth day of the month,
the ark came to rest on the mountains of Ararat."

In the Babylonian epic, at the end of the flood, the boat of Utnapishtim lodged firm on Mount Nimush.
In the Babylonian Epic of Gilgamesh, we read:
"The boat lodged firm On Mount Nimush."

The Mesopotamian tablet: lines 131-143 describe how:
"The storm calmed down
and the ship rested firm on Mount Nisir."

*** *** ***

6.Destroying mankind:
In the Babylonian Genesis of Eridu, Tablet XI, line 98, we read:
"The gods decided that mankind shall be destroyed."

In the Bible, Genesis 6:13, we read:
"And God said to Noah,
I have determined to make an end of all flesh,
for the earth is filled with violence because of them;
now I am going to destroy them along with the earth."

27

Chapter 6, Genesis 6:7,
"So the Lord said, I will blot out from the earth
the human beings I have created
people together with animals and
creeping things and birds of the air,
for I am sorry that I have made them."

Chapter 6, Genesis 6:17,
"For my part, I am going to bring
a flood of waters on the earth,
to destroy from under heaven all flesh
in which is the breath of life;
everything that is on the earth shall die."

*** *** ***

7.Reason for sending the flood:

The Sumerian clay tablets told us that the Anunnaki sent the flood to annihilate mankind, because their noise (clamor) was disturbing their rest and sleep. But the Assyro-Babylonian texts told us in Tablet XI of the Epic of Gilgamesh, that the gods sent the flood because the people of the city of Shurippak were wicked and corrupt.

Hereby are excerpts from a dialogue between Gilgamesh and Utnapishtim (The Hebrew Noah).

Utnapishtim talking to Gilgamesh:
"I will reveal to you, O Gilgamesh,
the mysterious story,
and the mystery of the Anunna (The Gods).
The city of Shurippak,
as you know is located
on the bank of the Euphrates River.
This city was wicked (corrupt),
so that the Anunna (The gods) living within it
decided to bring a deluge."

This Assyrian version coincides with the Biblical story of the deluge in Genesis.

*** *** ***

8.Never again to bring a flood to earth and destroy mankind:

After the flood the Anunnaki gods decided to bring peace and safety to Earth, and the assembly of the Mesopotamian gods (The Anunnaki) promised to never again send a flood, and destroy the human race.

The Biblical story told us that after the flood, Yahweh blessed Noah and promised him to never again bring a flood and destroy mankind.

Genesis 9:15,
*"I will remember my covenant that is between me
and you and every living creature of all flesh;
and the waters shall never again become
a flood to destroy all flesh."*

Genesis 9:16,
*"When the bow is in the clouds,
I will see it and remember the everlasting covenant
between God and every living creature of
all flesh that is on the earth."*

Genesis 8:21,
*"And when the Lord smelled the pleasing odor,
the Lord said in his heart, I will never again
curse the ground because of humankind,
for the inclination of the human
heart is evil from youth;
nor will I ever again destroy every
living creature as I have done."*

However, there is a nuance's difference; the Anunnaki gods felt sorry for bringing the great flood, and many of them were in tears, because so many people were killed.

29

On a Babylonian slab, hundreds of years older than the Bible: The Sumerian-Akkadian Noah (Utnapishtim, Ziusudra) in his boat.

Per contra, Yahweh did not express any regret for bringing the great flood and annihilating humankind, because humans were wicked and deserved such a severe punishment.

*** *** ***

9.The 7th day of the flood:
In the Babylonian Atrahasis, we read: *"On the seventh day of the flood."*

In the Bible, Genesis 7:10,
"after seven days the waters of the flood came upon the earth." 7.10.

*** *** ***

10. Seven days of flood: In the Bible.
Genesis 7:14,
"For in seven days I will send rain on the earth
for forty days and forty nights;
and every living thing that I have made

I will blot out from the face of the ground."

*** *** ***

11. Waiting for the 7ᵗʰ day in the Babylonian text:
In the Babylonian Epic of Gilgamesh, line 146, we read:

"And Utnapishtim, upon the seventh day."
In the Bible, Genesis 8:10, we read,
"He (Noah) waited another seven days..."

*** *** ***

12. Sealing the door and cover of the boat with pitch:
In the Babylonian text, we read,
"He (Utnapishtim) brought pitch to seal the door."
In the Bible, Genesis 6:14,
"Make yourself an ark of cypress wood;
make rooms in the ark, and cover it
inside and out with pitch."

The body of Utnapishtim's boat and Noah's Ark (The chassis if you want) were coated (Covered, painted, sealed) with the same material. It is called "Pitch".
The Biblical ark of Noah was coated with pitch and tar.
The Babylonian boat was coated (Sealed) with pitch and bitumen, basically and essential the same coating. Bitumen and tar were the very same material in ancient times.
In the Mesopotamian tablet: The ship of Utnapishtim was sealed with tar (Bitumen).
In the Bible: The boat (Ark) of Noah was sealed with tar.

*** *** ***

13. Making a roof (Cover for the boat) in the Babylonian text:
In the Babylonian Atrahasis, we read:
"Make a roof (Cover) over the boat like the Apsu."

31

In the Bible, Genesis 6:14,
"Make yourself an ark of cypress wood;
make rooms in the ark, and cover it
inside and out with pitch."
In the Bible, Genesis 6:16,
"Make a roof for the ark, and finish it
to a cubit above; and put the door of the ark
in its side; make it with lower, second,
and third decks."

*** *** ***

14. The covenant:
In the Babylonian Epic of Gilgamesh, line 165, we read,
"I (Utnapishtim) will remember those days,
and I will never forget them."

In the Bible, Genesis 6:18,
"But I will establish my covenant with you;
and you shall come into the ark,
you, your sons, your wife, and
your sons' wives with you."

In the Bible, Chapter 9, Genesis 9:9, we read,
"As for me, I am establishing my covenant with you
and your descendants after you."

Chapter 9, Genesis 9:10,
"And with every living creature that is with you,
the birds, the domestic animals,
and every animal of the earth with you,
as many as came out of the ark."

Chapter 9, Genesis 9:11,
"I establish my covenant with you,
that never again shall all flesh be cut off
by the waters of a flood,
and never again shall there be
a flood to destroy the earth."

Chapter 9, Genesis 9:12,
"God said, This is the sign of the covenant
that I make between me and
you and every living creature that is with you,
for all future generations."

*** *** ***

15.Offerings and sacrifices:
In the Babylonian Epic of Gilgamesh, lines 156 and 160, we read:
"I (Utnapishtim) sacrificed offerings
and I burned incense,
and the gods smelled the odor
and were pleased."

The Mesopotamian tablet: Lines 156-161:
Utnapishtim made an offering
to the gods on the mountain,
which pleased them enormously.

In a Babylonian-Assyrian version of the story of the flood, Ziusudra sacrificed an ox and a sheep to the gods.
In the Bible, Noah made a sacrifice to god Yahweh.

Chapter 8, Genesis 8:20,
"Then Noah built an altar to the Lord,
and took of every clean animal
and of every clean bird,
and offered burnt offerings on the altar."

In the Bible, Genesis 8:21, we read,
"And when the Lord smelled the pleasing odor..."

*** *** ***

16.The blessing of Utnapishtim and Noah:
The Mesopotamian tablet: Lines 178-188:
"God Enlil went aboard the ship

33

and blessed Utnapishtim and his wife."

In the Babylonian Epic of Gilgamesh, line 201, we read,
"He (god) blessed us."

In the Bible, god Yahweh too blessed Noah and his family.
In the Bible, Genesis 9:1,
"God blessed Noah and his sons,
and said to them, Be fruitful and multiply,
and fill the earth."

Chapter 9, Genesis 9:7,
"And you, be fruitful and multiply,
abound on the earth and multiply in it."

***   ***   ***

Characteristics and dissimilarities of the three Babylonian versions of the story of the flood, the Epic of Gilgamesh and Berossus' account.

The Babylonian stories of the flood shared some resemblance with the Epic of Gilgamesh.
But the clay tablets from Ashurbanipal's library in Nineveh originated at a much later period.
A second (newer) Assyrian story of the flood differs from the Epic of Gilgamesh.
In the first and earlier version, Utnapishtim was the main character.
In a newer version, Atrahasis became the leading character. Utnapishtim of the Gilgamesh Epic, in lines 54 to 79 appeared to be a seasoned ship-builder.

In the second Assyrian version, in lines 11 to 17, Atrahasis was depicted as an inexperienced ship-builder, and begged god Ea to draw a design of the boat, so he could build one.

In the first and earliest version of the story of the flood: (First Dynasty of Babylon, circa 1844-1505 B.C.), the larger animals and birds were to be saved, and brought to the boat. The gods asked Utnapishtim to give a name to the boat which would save him and his family.
In the second Babylonian story of the Flood, written or copied in the 11th year of the reign of King Ammisaduqa, when he rebuilt Dur-Ammi-saduqa, the main character is Utnapishtim.
Utnapishtim built a ship but left behind all his possessions. Worth mentioning here that Atramhasis is an Old Babylonian form for the later Assyrian Atrahasis. In one version of the story, Ziusudra was saved in a boat during the deluge, which lasted seven days. When Ziusudra opened the roof's cover, Utu the sun god appeared to him. After he sacrificed an ox and a sheep, and bowed before Enlil and Anu, Ziusudra received the gift of immortality in Dilmun (Modern day Bahrain).

The Sumerian story of the flood according to Berossus, a priest of the cult of Marduk in Babylon.

Around 275 B.C., Berossus, a contemporary of the king Antiochus I Soter (281-260), wrote in Greek a history of Babylon titled "Babyloniaca".
Unfortunately, his book was lost.

However, few passages from the book were quoted by:
- a-Georgius Syncellus (circa A.D. 792 A.D.),
- b-Eusebius of Caesarea (A.D. 265-340 A.D.),
- c-Flavius Josephus 37-103 A.D.),
- d-King Juba of Mauretania (circa 50 B.C.-23 A.D.),
- e-Alexander Polyhistor (circa 88 B.C.),
- f-Apollodorus of Athens (circa 144 B.C.)

Berossus' story of the flood remained the only and first Babylonian account of the deluge, before the cuneiform clay tablets of Nineveh were discovered. In his story, one of the gods warned Xisuthros of the Flood, and instructed him to build a boat to save his life, his family and friends, and animals.
After the flood, Xisuthros disembarked on a mountain in Armenia. And the gods granted him immortality, and joined the gods.
Worth noting that the names of Ziusudra and Xisuthros appeared both in the account of Berossus and in the Sumerian clay tablet of the flood.

*** *** ***

The Babylonian story of the Flood and the Biblical account of the Deluge were mentioned on a tablet from Ugarit.

In 1960, Jean Nougayrol announced to the world, the discovery of a fragment of an Ugaritic tablet mentioning the Mesopotamian flood. It contained twenty lines and started with the following:
"When the gods counseled together,
the flood came to the countries."

The remaining 18 lines were similar to passages from Tablet XI (7th century B.C.) of the Babylonian Assyrian version from the library of Ashurbanipal found in Nineveh however a few sections differed from the Ugaritic tablet; here are some examples:

In The Assyro-Babylonian version, Utnapishtim (The Hebrew Noah) is listening to god Ea, from his house in Shuruppak. Ea told Utnapishtim about the Flood.
In the Ugaritic tablet, Utnapishtim was not at home, but in the temple of god Ea who promised to save him and to grant him immortality.
However, what Ea told Utnapishtim in the Assyro-Babylonian version is similar to to what it was recorded on the Ugaritic fragmented tablet, and began in this manner: "Wall, hear!"

Recent Books by Maximillien de Lafayette

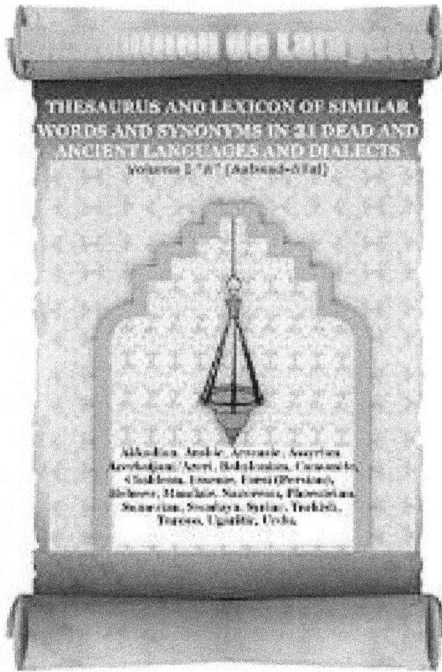

THESAURUS AND LEXICON OF SIMILAR WORDS AND SYNONYMS IN 21 DEAD AND ANCIENT LANGUAGES AND DIALECTS

A set of 20 volumes. THESAURUS & LEXICON OF SIMILAR WORDS & SYNONYMS IN 21 DEAD & ANCIENT LANGUAGES AND DIALECTS.

Akkadian, Arabic, Aramaic, Assyrian, Azerbaijani/Azeri, Babylonian, Canaanite, Chaldean, Essenic, Farsi (Persian), Hebrew, Mandaic, Nazorean, Phoenician, Sumerian, Swadaya, Syriac, Turkish, Turoyo, Ugaritic, Urdu.

The world's 1st dictionary/thesaurus/lexicon of its kind! A gem. A literary treasure! Written by the world's most prolific linguist who authored 21 dictionaries of dead and ancient languages known to mankind. Published by Times Square Press NY.

Maximillien de Lafayette

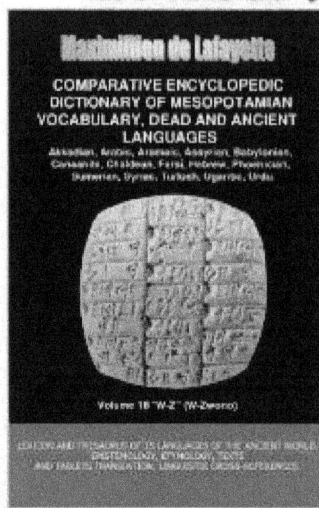

COMPARATIVE ENCYCLOPEDIC
DICTIONARY OF MESOPOTAMIAN
VOCABULARY, DEAD AND ANCIENT
LANGUAGES

Akkadian, Arabic, Aramaic, Assyrian, Babylonian,
Canaanite, Chaldean, Farsi, Hebrew, Phoenician,
Sumerian, Syriac, Turkish, Ugaritic, Urdu

Volume 18 "W-Z" (W-Zwano)

LEXICON AND THESAURUS OF 15 LANGUAGES OF THE ANCIENT WORLD
EPISTEMOLOGY, ETYMOLOGY, TEXTS
AND TABLETS TRANSLATION, LINGUISTIC CROSS-REFERENCES

**Comparative Encyclopedic Dictionary of
Mesopotamian Vocabulary, Dead and Ancient
Languages. Lexicon and Thesaurus of 15
Languages and Dialects of the Ancient World**
A set of 18 volumes (Approximately 4,200 pages).

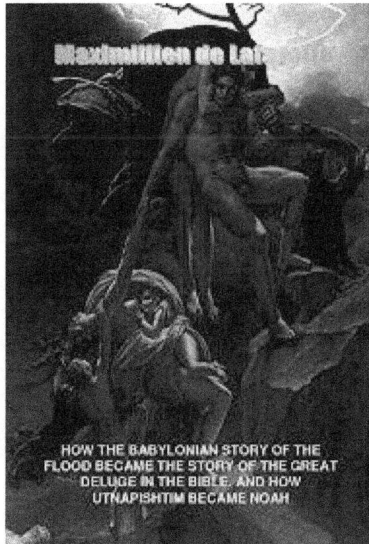

How the Babylonian Story of the Flood Became the Story of the Great Deluge in the Bible. And How Utnapishtim Became Noah.

From the content:
• Biblical stories taken from much older religions.
• The Babylonian Story of the Flood Versus the Biblical Story of the Flood.
• There is a difference of approximately 600 years between the Babylonian flood and the Biblical flood.
• Excerpts from the Mesopotamian texts, word-for-word, and my translation.
• Same stories in the Babylonian texts and the Bible:
• 1.The Anunnaki god Ea warned Utnapishtim about a flood.
• Instructions on how to build the boat.
• 2.Bringing animals to the boat.
• 3.The dove.
• 4.The birds are set free.
• 5.The boat resting on the top of a mountain.
• 6.Destroying mankind.
• 7.Reason for sending the flood.
• 8.Never again to bring a flood to earth and destroy

mankind.
- 9.The 7th day of the flood.
- 10. Seven days of flood: In the Bible.
- 11.Waiting for the 7th day.
- 12.Sealing the door and cover of the boat with pitch.
- 13.Making a roof (Cover for the boat).
- 14.The covenant.
- 15.Offerings and sacrifices.
- 16.The blessing of Utnapishtim and Noah.
- Characteristics and dissimilarities of the three Babylonian versions of the story of the flood, the Epic of Gilgamesh and Berossus' account.
- The Sumerian story of the flood according to Berossus, a priest of the cult of Marduk in Babylon.

———————————————

Published by
TIMES SQUARE PRESS, NEW YORK
www.timessquarepress.com

www.ingramcontent.com/pod-product-compliance
Lightning Source LLC
Chambersburg PA
CBHW030308030426
42337CB00012B/629